This paper is part of the Proceedings of the First North-American Conference on Semitic Linguistics Santa Barbara, California March 24-25, 1973

I0883214

PHONOLOGICAL CHANNELS IN CHAHA

C. Douglas Johnson
University of California, Santa Barbara

In Chaha the impersonal and Sg. 3m. object suffixes labialize the nearest preceding plain noncoronal consonant. Furthermore a consonant will become identical to the next following consonant if it can do so by becoming labialized or palatalized. An attempt to formulate these rules in an economical way that reflects universal constraints on action at a distance leads to the proposal that the notation X_0 be abolished from generative phonology and that in its stead there be used structural descriptions of the more restricted form [X [Y] [Z]], having the meaning of $[X, Y] [-X]_0 [X, Z]$.

TABLE OF CONTENTS

0. THEORETICAL SETTING

Chomsky and Halle (1968) base their phonological formalism upon a minimal feature system and a few very general and powerful operators, notably braces and subscripts. To take care of a few marginal cases they go so far as to introduce transformational machinery. They and others (Chomsky and Halle 1968:427, McCawley 1971) have recognized the empirical inadequacy of this approach. On the one hand the Chomsky-Halle formalism is excessively powerful, being able to express a vast array of phonologically impossible or implausible rules, even in a simple way; on the other hand it fails to provide intuitively satisfying formulations for many quite common phonological rules. The cited authors suggest that the remedy is to replace the small set of extremely general devices with a probably larger set of more specifically phonological ones. I would like here to make some specific proposals in this direction, focusing on the evidence of two phonological rules of Chaha,[1] an Ethiopian Semitic language of the Gurage group.

1. THE FACTS OF CHAHA

The rules of interest concern the palatalization and labialization of Chaha consonants.

1.1. The Chaha Consonant System

These secondary articulations, which arise largely but not entirely by rule, superimpose themselves upon three basic places of articulation definable in terms of the lower articulator. The resulting surface system of consonants is essentially that shown in Table I.

Labial	Plain	*p*	b, β		*m*		*f*	
	Labialized	p^w	b^w		m^w		f^w	
Coronal	Plain	*t*	*d*	*ṭ*	*n*	*r*	*s*	z
	Palatalized	č	ǧ	č̣			š	ž
Dorsal	Plain	*k*	*g*	*q*			x	
	Palatalized	k^y	g^w	q^w			x^w	
	Labialized	k^w	g^w	q^w			x^w	

TABLE I. Chaha consonantism. C̣ =ejective, q =ḳ

In addition there are two semivowels *w* and *y* and a marginal *ℓ* and *p̣*. Postvocalic *b* and b^w regularly become β and *w*, respectively, and this is the only source of β (Polotsky 1951:13, Leslau 1967:1157); cf. the following forms of the verb *bäna-* 'eat':

[1] The material on which this paper is based has been drawn chiefly from Leslau (1950, 1966, 1967, 1967-8) and Polotsky (1951). In addition Robert Hetzron has very kindly provided me with data from his own unpublished notes and observations. He has offered invaluable comments and advice concerning the interpretation of facts discussed here, but does not necessarily agree with everything I say and is in no way responsible for my errors.

	perfect	impersonal
perfect[2]	*bäna* 'he ate'	*bʷäne* 'one ate it'
imperfect	*yəβära* 'he eats'	*yəwäre* 'one eats it'

There are, however, exceptions to this rule; e.g. the second radical of certain verb roots is an invariant *b*; cf. *ṭäbäṭä-* 'seize'.[3]

It can be seen that not all of the possibilities of secondary articulation are realized. Labials, *n* and *r* cannot be palatalized and coronals cannot be labialized. The secondary articulations have certain expected concomitants. The plain dorsals, coronals, and labials are ordinary velars, dentals, and bilabials, respectively, the labial fricative being however labiodental. A palatalized dorsal is a palatal or a fronted velar, but is otherwise like its plain counterpart. A palatalized coronal, on the other hand, is a strident palato-alveolar with delayed release, so that the palatalized counterpart of *t*, for example, is not *tʸ*, but č.

1.2. Secondary Articulations as Exponents of Grammatical Categories

1.2.1. PALATALIZATION

Palatalization occurs as a mark of certain grammatical categories. The second person singular feminine subject (2SFS) suffix, in particular, has no overt realization of its own but palatalizes the last consonant of the verb root if that consonant is palatalizable. Paired masculine and feminine forms of the singular imperative illustrate the effect:

MASCULINE	FEMININE	
gäkət	*gäkəč*	'accompany'
nəmäd	*nəmäǧ*	'love'
nəqəṭ	*nəqəč̣*	'kick'
nəkəs	*nəkəš*	'bite'
zarg	*zargʸ*	'leave'
gəräz	*gəräž*	'be old'
wətäq	*wətäqʸ*	'fall'
fəräx	*fəräxʸ*	'be patient'

[2]Perfects must take a suffixal *-m* when they function as the verb of a nonnegated main clause. This suffix, which must follow all of the subject and object pronominal suffixes, is omitted throughout the paper as irrelevant. Hence the perfects actually cited are subordinate forms.

[3]Because of these exceptions *b* and β must be regarded as separate autonomous phonemes. Nevertheless Leslau and Polotsky usually transcribe both sounds as *b* when citing forms and presenting texts. Robert Hetzron has been able to provide or confirm unambiguous transcriptions for the forms cited in this paper. It might be thought that in a generative phonology *b* ought to underlie invariant *b* and that β out to be the source of the *b*~β alternation, the rule being that nonpostvocalic β becomes *b*. We have rejected this alternative because phonetic β seems to behave like a stop in the morphology; cf. the behavior of the second radical in the following perfect/imperfect pairs: *wäka/yəwäga* 'crush', *gačä/yəgaǧ* 'tie up the feet', *bätärä/yəβädər* 'be ahead of', *qäpärä/yəqäβər* 'bury'. Furthermore the exceptional cases where *b* fails to spirantize seem to fall into a few well-defined types partly of foreign origin (Leslau 1967:1157). The exact manner of handling these exceptions is not crucial to the issues discussed here.

1.2.2. LABIALIZATION

Labialization too occurs as an exponent of certain grammatical elements. The third person singular masculine object (3MSO) affix, for example, manifests itself as *n* in the appropriate suffixal position and simultaneously labializes the nearest preceding plain noncoronal consonant. The following perfects (subordinate forms) illustrate the phenomenon:

OBJECTLESS	WITH 3MSO	
sädädä	*sädädän*	'chase'
dänägä	*dänäg*^{w}*än*	'hit'
nädäfä	*nädäf*^{w}*än*	'sting'
qänäfä	*qänäf*^{w}*än*	'knock down'
näkäβä	*näkäwän*	'find'
šäfärä	*šäf*^{w}*ärän*	'cover'
näkäsä	*näk*^{w}*äsän*	'bite'
käfätä	*käf*^{w}*ätän*	'open'
bäkärä	*bäk*^{w}*ärä*	'lack'
qäṭärä	*q*^{w}*äṭärän*	'kill'
mäsärä	*m*^{w}*äsärän*	'seem'
mäk^{y}*ärä*	*m*^{w}*äk*^{y}*ärän*	'burn'

1.2.3. JOINT PALATALIZATION AND LABIALIZATION

The impersonal form induces both labialization and palatalization; cf. the following subordinate perfects (the final palatal vowel is a Sg. 3m. object suffix allomorph e.g. *q*^{w}*äṭär-i* 'one killed him' ~ 'he was killed', cf. *q*^{w}*äṭär-kä* 'one killed you (m.sg.)' ~ 'you were killed'):

PERSONAL (Sg. 3m.)	IMPERSONAL	
täg^{y}*äna*	*täg*^{y}*äne*	'cross over'
g^{y}*äk*^{y}*ärä*	*g*^{y}*äk*^{y}*äri*	'straighten out'
täg^{y}*ag*^{y}*äzä*	*täg*^{y}*ag*^{y}*äži*	'be haughty'
anṭä	*anč̣i*	'cut'
bätäxä	*bätäx*^{w}*i*	'dig out'
näkäβä	*näkäwi*	'find'
šägärä	*šäg*^{w}*äri*	'change'
näkäsä	*näk*^{w}*äši*	'bite'
käfätä	*käf*^{w}*äči*	'open'
bänärä	*b*^{w}*änäri*	'demolish'
qäṭärä	*q*^{w}*äṭäri*	'kill'

1.3. Harmony in Secondary Articulation

By a process of CONSONANT HARMONY a consonant will also acquire a secondary articulation if it will thereby become identical to the next following consonant. Consequently, if the last two consonants of a root are identical they will both become palatalized in the feminine of the second person singular imperative:

MASCULINE	FEMININE	
bätət	*bäčəč*	'be wide'
ädəd	*äǧəǧ*	'cut peas or lentils'
fäṭəṭ	*fäč̣əč̣*	'be partial'
äsəs	*äšəš*	'sweep'
nəzäz	*nəžäž*	'dream'
nəqəq	*nəqʸəqʸ*	'take apart'
səkək	*səkʸəkʸ*	'plant in the ground'

Observe, however, that the feminine of *ṭəbṭ* 'seize' is *ṭəbč̣*, not **č̣əbč̣*. The intervening *b* blocks the spread of palatalization from the last to the first *ṭ*.

Similarly, a consonant will become labialized if it can thereby become identical to the next following consonant. That is the reason for the double labialization in the second of the following pairs of perfects:

OBJECTLESS	WITH 3SMO	
akäkä	*akʷäkʷän*	'scratch'
aṭäqäqä	*aṭäqʷäqʷän*	'soften'

The impersonal formation illustrates harmony in both palatalization and labialization:

PERSONAL	IMPERSONAL	
tata	*čače*	'twist a rope'
aṭaṭa	*ač̣ač̣e*	'rinse'
näzäzä	*nážäži*	'dream'
kʸäsäsä	*kʸäšäši*	'accuse'
säkäkä	*säkʷäkʷi*	'plant in the ground'
gämämä	*gämʷämʷi*	'chip the rim'
məräqäqä	*məräqʷäqʷi*	'scratch in a straight line'
bərägägä	*bərägʷägʷi*	'be startled'

The personal/impersonal pairs *zasa/zaše* 'act mad' and *žəβapärä/žəwapʷäri* 'turn upside down' can be explained on the assumption of the underlying stems *zazza-* and *žəbabbär-*, respectively. There being no phonetic geminate consonants in Chaha, it is possible to postulate rules (which in fact reflect historical changes) that devoice and degeminate double obstruents. If it is further assumed that consonant harmony applies iteratively from right to left, as predicted by two recently proposed theories (Howard 1972, Jensen and Stong-Jensen 1973), then the verb forms in question can be derived approximately as follows:

zazza	*zažže*	*žəbabbärä*	*zəbabbʷäri*	impersonal palatalization & labialization
	žažže		*žəbʷabʷbʷäri*	consonant harmony
zassa	*žašše*	*žəbappärä*	*žəbʷapʷpʷäri*	devoicing
zasa	*žaše*	*žəbapärä*	*žəbʷapʷäri*	degemination
		žəβapärä	*žəβʷapʷäri*	spirantization
			žəwapʷäri	βʷ → w

2. FORMALIZATION

2.1. Feature Representation of Secondary Articulations

We now seek an optional formalization of the consonant harmony and labialization rules. As a preliminary we must establish a feature representation for secondary articulations. Ideally the feature system should reflect the fact that the number of distinct secondary articulations in any language is universally quite limited, there being perhaps at the most three in addition to plain articulation. Recall furthermore that the Chaha labialization rule, triggered by the 3SMO suffix and the impersonal suffix, refers to the class of plain consonants. This class appears to be a natural one that ought to be represented by a conjunction of feature specifications. The older features [flat] and [sharp] would serve these purposes admirably, since they could designate the class of plain consonants as [-flat, -sharp] and imply a maximum of three secondary articulations.

The secondary articulations, however, are closely allied with the various vowel qualities, and indeed often arise by assimilation to them. These considerations as well as a return to articulatory terminology led Chomsky and Halle to abandon the [flat] and [sharp] features and to use the vowel quality features directly to specify secondary articulations. This approach, however, conflicts with the requirements set forth above. It implies, unless some further restriction is built into the theory, that there can be as many secondary articulations (counting the plain articulations) as vowel qualities. Furthermore, since palatalized consonants must be referred to as [-back, +high], the natural class of plain consonants can be represented only by means of a disjunction:

$$\begin{bmatrix} -\text{round} \\ \left\{ \begin{matrix} +\text{back} \\ -\text{high} \end{matrix} \right\} \end{bmatrix}$$

As an interim solution to this dilemma I will introduce a nonprimitive feature of palatalization, relevant only to consonants but defined in terms of the primitive vowel quality features of backness and rounding. [+palatalized] is thus defined universally as [-back, +high]. The meaning of [-palatalized] depends on other features of the consonant. A nonanterior noncoronal nonpalatalized consonant is by definition [+back], while an anterior nonpalatalized consonant is [-high].

2.2. Formalization of Consonant Harmony

2.1.1. STANDARD NOTATION

Consider now the rule of consonant harmony. The ordinary slash/dash notation of Chomsky and Halle requires mention of a large set of features in order to specify the required identity between the consonants, leading to a formulation like (1).

$$(1) \quad \begin{bmatrix} -\text{syl} \\ \alpha\text{ant} \\ \beta\text{cor} \\ \gamma\text{cont} \\ \delta\text{nas} \\ \varepsilon\text{voice} \\ \zeta\text{glot} \end{bmatrix} \rightarrow \begin{bmatrix} \eta\text{back} \\ \theta\text{pal} \end{bmatrix} \Big/ \text{----}[+\text{syl}]_0 \begin{bmatrix} -\text{syl} \\ \alpha\text{ant} \\ \beta\text{cor} \\ \gamma\text{cont} \\ \delta\text{nas} \\ \varepsilon\text{voice} \\ \zeta\text{glot} \\ \eta\text{back} \\ \theta\text{pal} \end{bmatrix}$$

2.2.2. TRANSFORMATIONAL FORMAT

Transformational format, however, if used in a slightly new way, can achieve a more insightful formulation of the identity condition:

$$\text{(2)}\quad \text{SD:}\quad \underset{1}{[-\text{syl}]},\quad \underset{2}{[+\text{syl}]_0},\quad \underset{3}{\begin{bmatrix} 1 \\ \alpha\text{round} \\ \beta\text{pal} \end{bmatrix}}$$

$$\text{SC:}\quad 1\ 2\ 3 \rightarrow 3\ 2\ 3$$

The only possible unorthodoxy in this formulation is the appearance of the expression

$$\begin{bmatrix} 1 \\ \alpha\text{round} \\ \beta\text{pal} \end{bmatrix}$$

in the structural description. When segment brackets contain numeral variables they usually appear in the structural change. In any case the meaning of the above expression is the same as if it appeared in the structural change; it means 'the [αround, βpalatalized] counterpart of term 1'.

2.2.3. SLASH/DASH NOTATION WITH SEGMENT VARIABLES

Though transformational format lends particular elegance to formulations such as (2) it is far too powerful for the restricted purposes of phonology, a fact that has been pointed out by a number of authors (Chomsky and Halle 1968:427-8; Johnson 1970:57). This great power derives in large part from the free use of numerals to identify pieces of a structural description; so used the numerals amount to general string variables. But those phonological rules which appear to require transformational machinery often do so only because they require variables ranging over segments. Accordingly I would propose, adapting suggestions of Postal 1969 and Johnson 1970, that variables be allowed only inside segment brackets in conjunction with the ordinary slash/dash notation. The rule of consonant harmony, then, will be revised as in (3).

$$\text{(3)}\quad \begin{bmatrix} 1 \\ -\text{syl} \end{bmatrix} \rightarrow \begin{bmatrix} \alpha\text{round} \\ \beta\text{pal} \end{bmatrix} \Big/ \ \text{----}\ [+\text{syl}]_0 \begin{bmatrix} 1 \\ -\text{syl} \\ \alpha\text{round} \\ \beta\text{pal} \end{bmatrix}$$

2.2.4. REUNITED STRUCTURAL DESCRIPTION

Still, by repeating a number of features that were mentioned only once in (2), this formulation loses something that was captured by the transformational format. Repetition has usually been regarded as a symptom of misanalysis, and indeed the abhorrence of repetition seems to have motivated a great many theoretical proposals in phonology. Observed consistently, this criterion would eventually lead to a formalism that eliminated all nonaccidental repetitions from the abbreviated versions of phonological rules and thereby make predictions about what sorts of repetitions could occur in the unabbreviated versions. This line of argument might suggest that transformational format ought to be reconsidered, but I will claim instead that the repetitions in (3) belong to a few general types which recur frequently throughout the world's languages and call for special devices that have nothing to do with transformational machinery. The formalization of these devices will proceed more smoothly if the structural descriptions of rules are reunited in the form adopted by Stanley (1967:412). Accordingly (3) will be recast as (4).

(4)

$$\begin{array}{ccc} \begin{bmatrix} 1 \\ -\text{syl} \end{bmatrix} & [+\text{syl}]_0 & \begin{bmatrix} 1 \\ -\text{syl} \\ \alpha\text{round} \\ \beta\text{pal} \end{bmatrix} \\ \downarrow & & \\ \begin{bmatrix} \alpha\text{round} \\ \beta\text{pal} \end{bmatrix} & & \end{array}$$

2.2.5. DISCONTINUOUS CHANNEL

If the consonant harmony rule could pretend that the vowels in the input string didn't exist it would reduce to a simple assimilation of contiguous segments:

(5)

$$\begin{array}{cc} [1] & \begin{bmatrix} 1 \\ \alpha\text{round} \\ \beta\text{pal} \end{bmatrix} \\ \downarrow & \\ \begin{bmatrix} \alpha\text{round} \\ \beta\text{pal} \end{bmatrix} & \end{array}$$

This formulation would, for example, correctly handle *bätəč* if the latter were regarded as a vowelless string *btč*.

At present the instruction to disregard vowels is incorporated into rule (4) as the repetitious configuration $[-\text{syl}][+\text{syl}]_0[-\text{syl}]$. To better capture the intuitive content of disregarding all vowels and at the same time to eliminate the repeated mentions of the feature [syllabic], we will reformulate the rule so that it operates on a DISCONTINUOUS CONSONANT CHANNEL. The proposed notation places the channel designation, in this case "-syllabic," above the basic structural description and encloses the whole in an outer pair of brackets. The consonant harmony rule then takes the following form:

(6)

$$\begin{array}{c} \begin{bmatrix} -\text{syl} & \\ [1] & \begin{bmatrix} 1 \\ \alpha\text{round} \\ \beta\text{pal} \end{bmatrix} \end{bmatrix} \\ \downarrow \\ \begin{bmatrix} \alpha\text{round} \\ \beta\text{pal} \end{bmatrix} \end{array}$$

To translate this back into previously known notation the relevant interpretive convention copies the channel designation into all of the explicitly mentioned segments in the structural description and then places zero-subscripted negated versions of the channel designation between and around those segments:

$$\begin{array}{ccccc} [+\text{syl}]_0 & \begin{bmatrix} 1 \\ -\text{syl} \end{bmatrix} & [+\text{syl}]_0 & \begin{bmatrix} 1 \\ -\text{syl} \\ \alpha\text{round} \\ \beta\text{pal} \end{bmatrix} & [+\text{syl}]_0 \\ & \downarrow & & & \\ & \begin{bmatrix} \alpha\text{round} \\ \beta\text{pal} \end{bmatrix} & & & \end{array}$$

Since zero-subscripted expressions at the extreme ends of a structural description are vacuous, this is logically equivalent to (4).

The discontinuous channel is not just an ad hoc device for handling Chaha consonant harmony. It is a partial solution to the general problem (raised, for example, by Kiparsky [1968:37-8]), of formulating rules that ignore "irrelevant" segments. There are plenty of such rules which achieve a near optimum form if they are provided with discontinuous channel designations. Most rules of umlaut, vowel harmony, and tone sandhi, for example, can be thought of as operating on a discontinuous vowel channel. The Chumash sibilant harmony rule (Beeler 1970), which causes a sibilant to assimilate in anteriority to a next following sibilant, operates on a discontinuous sibilant channel. The Latin rule which changes *l* in the morpheme *-ālis* to *r* when the next preceding liquid is *l* is operating in a discontinuous liquid channel.

2.2.6. CONTINUOUS CHANNEL

Repetition of the variable "1," which still remains, can also be eliminated by a cross-linguistically well motivated device. Consider the fact that many rules which don't operate on a discontinuous channel nevertheless demand that the contiguous segments in their structural descriptions share some phonological property. Ukrainian, for example, has a rule of sibilant harmony that affects only contiguous segments, although it is otherwise identical to the Chumash rule. This rule might be said to operate on a CONTINUOUS sibilant channel. A rule that assimilates the voicing of one obstruent to the voicing of the immediately following one is operating on a consonant harmony rule if all of the segments lying outside that rule's discontinuous channel (i.e. the vowels) are set aside. For then the rule is seen to operate on a continuous IDENTITY channel.

We will place continuous channel designations in a separate pair of brackets lying above and coinciding in horizontal extent with the basic structural description. Thus Chaha consonant harmony is now to be formulated as follows:

$$(7)\qquad \begin{array}{l} \begin{bmatrix} \begin{array}{c} \text{-syl} \\ [\qquad 1 \qquad] \\ [\quad\;\;] \begin{bmatrix} \alpha\text{round} \\ \beta\text{pal} \end{bmatrix} \end{array} \end{bmatrix} \\ \quad\;\; \downarrow \\ \begin{bmatrix} \alpha\text{round} \\ \beta\text{pal} \end{bmatrix} \end{array}$$

The relevant interpretive convention simply copies the continuous channel designation into the segments mentioned in the structural description. This convention applies before the discontinuous channel convention, yielding (6).

2.2.7. ASSIMILATORY ARROW

There is one last obvious move. A rule that causes one segment to assimilate in certain features to another segment must mention those features both in the conditioning segment and in the structural change. This repetition can be eliminated by placing some mark, say a downward pointing arrow, by the side of the assimiliatory feature(s) in the conditioning segment, provided that the segment to be changed can be uniquely identified. This is frequently possible because so many assimilatory rules mention only two segments. Futhermore many apparent exceptions, rules which on the face of it mention more than two segments, reduce to two-segment form under the discontinuous channel convention.

Chaha consonant harmony is just such a rule and we propose therefore to write it as follows:

(8) $$\begin{bmatrix} -\text{syl} \\ [\quad 1 \quad] \\ \begin{bmatrix} \quad \end{bmatrix} \begin{bmatrix} \downarrow \alpha\text{round} \\ \beta\text{pal} \end{bmatrix} \end{bmatrix}$$

2.3. Palatoalveolarization

As we noted earlier, every palatalized coronal in Chaha is a strident palato-alveolar with delayed release. These supplementary effects were not included in the universal definition of [+palatalized] because they do not invariably accompany palatalized coronals in all languages (e.g. Russian has palatalized dental stops), and the question arises as to how then to introduce these effects in Chaha. Chomsky and Halle (1968:421-2) propose marking conventions that automatically turn palatalized coronals into strident palatoalveolars unless there is some language specific block, but these conventions don't apply to any of the outputs of a rule unless it can apply to all of the outputs of that rule (p. 431.). Hence the conventions under consideration would not be set in motion by Chaha consonant harmony because that rule affects consonants at all places of articulation and labializes as well as palatalizes. On the other hand if the all-or-none principle were dropped the palatalized velars would incorrectly become strident palatoalveolars too because they should first of all become coronal according to the marking conventions. The only way to block this coronalization and consequent strident palatoalveolarization would be to incorporate the subrule [αcoronal]→[αcoronal] into ALL rules having a palatalizing effect on velars. Since Chaha has several such rules in addition to consonant harmony (e.g. 2SFS palatalization), this approach would have to repeat the same generalization at several different places in the grammar, and seems therefore to be incorrect.

Presumably, then, Chaha has its own palatoalveolarization rule making all [+high, +coronal] consonants [-anterior, -delayed release, +strident]. If this rule is a late phonetic one, the feminine of *bätət*, for example, is derived by the steps *bätət^y* (2SFS palatalization), *bät^y ət^y* (consonant harmony), *bäčəč* (palatoalveolarizaiton). Alternatively, the Chaha palatoalveolarization rule might be some sort of language specific addendum to the definition of [+palatalized] rather than a phonological rule in the ordinary sense. Then *bäčəč* would be derived from *bätət*+2SFS more directly in two steps: *bätəč* (2SFS palatalization), *bäčəč* (consonant harmony).

2.4. Formalization of Labialization

We turn next to labilization, the rule whereby the impersonal and the 3SMO suffixes labialize the nearest preceding plain labializable consonant. Polotsky (1951:24-26) has pointed out that *ŭ* has no phonetic existence in Chaha except in the neighborhood of a velar, and there it seems to be derived by a low-level optional rule K^wə→Kŭ, where K is a velar. Hence it is possible to assume that the suffixes here in question contain an underlying *ŭ* which induces the labialization of the appropriate consonant and then disappears. Since *ĭ* too seems to have no independent existence on the phonetic level (*i* exists but is derived from *əy* or *əĭ*; cf. Polotsky 1951:18-24) it can be posited as the palatalizing element in the 2SFS and impersonal suffixes (the impersonal then would contain both *ŭ* and *ĭ*). This *ĭ* too disappears on the phonetic level. Hence there seems to be an independent rule deleting short high vowels, and the deletion of the *ŭ* does not therefore have to be effected by the labialization rule itself. The labialization rule can therefore be regarded as a kind of assimilation, the *ŭ* transmitting its rounding to the nearest preceding plain noncoronal consonant.

Using the ordinary slash/dash notation we would, then, formulate the labialization rule as follows:

$$(9)\quad \begin{bmatrix} -\text{syl} \\ -\text{cor} \\ -\text{round} \\ -\text{pal} \end{bmatrix} \rightarrow [+\text{round}] \Bigg/ \text{----} \left[\left\{ \begin{matrix} +\text{syl} \\ +\text{cor} \\ +\text{round} \\ +\text{pal} \end{matrix} \right\} \right]_0 \begin{bmatrix} +\text{syl} \\ +\text{high} \\ -\text{long} \\ +\text{round} \end{bmatrix}$$

But this formulation not only repeats several features but employs both subscript zeroes and braces, both of which are probably far too powerful for phonology in their unrestricted form. Some authors (McCawley 1971, Anderson 1972) have claimed indeed that one or both of the devices could be entirely eliminated by a notation more closely tailored to the specific needs of phonology. The machinery developed here is offered as a contribution to such a notation and it will, in fact, eliminate the need for braces and subscript zeroes in many cases, as well as repetitions of features. The labialization rule in Chaha is a striking example of such a case, for now it can be reformulated in a way to meet virtually all of the objections raised above to formulation (9). This reformulation is:

$$(10)\quad \begin{bmatrix} -\text{syl} \\ -\text{cor} \\ -\text{round} \\ -\text{pal} \\ [\quad] \end{bmatrix} \begin{bmatrix} +\text{syl} \\ +\text{high} \\ -\text{long} \\ \downarrow +\text{round} \end{bmatrix}$$

To retranslate this back into the Chomsky-Halle format, the assimilatory feature convention will first create a structural change beneath the first segment of the structural description, copying into that change the feature specifications associated with the downward pointing arrow in the second segment of the structural description:

$$(11)\quad \underset{\substack{\downarrow \\ [+\text{round}]}}{\begin{bmatrix} -\text{syl} \\ -\text{cor} \\ -\text{round} \\ [\quad] \end{bmatrix}} \begin{bmatrix} +\text{syl} \\ +\text{high} \\ -\text{long} \\ +\text{round} \end{bmatrix}$$

The discontinuous channel convention converts this into the following:

---

[4]We have been assuming that a labializing suffix affects the nearest preceding PLAIN non-coronal consonant, in conformity with the example in Leslau (1967:1159):

tägmʷämʷätä	(personal)	'rinse'
tägʷmʷämʷäči	(impersonal)	

Hetzron (personal communication) disagrees with Leslau's phonetics and the consequent formulation of the labialization rule. He believes that the impersonal form of the cited verb is *tägmʷämʷäči* and that the labializing affixes round the nearest preceding NONPALATALIZED noncoronal consonant, whether the latter is already rounded or not. If Hetzron is correct the designation "-round" can simply be deleted from the discontinuous channel designation in (11). So modified the rule would vacuously round the second *mʷ* in *tägmʷämʷäči* and leave the plain *g* alone.

$$\left[\left\{\begin{matrix}\text{+syl}\\ \text{+cor}\\ \text{+round}\\ \text{+pal}\end{matrix}\right\}\right]_0 \underset{\substack{\downarrow\\ [\text{+round}]}}{\begin{bmatrix}\text{-syl}\\ \text{-cor}\\ \text{-round}\\ \text{-pal}\end{bmatrix}} \left[\left\{\begin{matrix}\text{+syl}\\ \text{+cor}\\ \text{+round}\\ \text{+pal}\end{matrix}\right\}\right]_0 \begin{bmatrix}\text{+syl}\\ \text{+high}\\ \text{-long}\\ \text{+round}\end{bmatrix}$$

Since zero-subscripted expressions on the extreme ends of a structural description are vacuous this formulation is logically equivalent to

$$\underset{\substack{\downarrow\\ [\text{+round}]}}{\begin{bmatrix}\text{-syl}\\ \text{-cor}\\ \text{-round}\\ \text{-pal}\end{bmatrix}} \left[\left\{\begin{matrix}\text{+syl}\\ \text{+cor}\\ \text{+round}\\ \text{+pal}\end{matrix}\right\}\right]_0 \begin{bmatrix}\text{+syl}\\ \text{+high}\\ \text{-long}\\ \text{+round}\end{bmatrix}$$

which is a notational variant of (9).

3. STATUS OF PROPOSED NOTATIONAL DEVICES

In this paper I have proposed and attempted to motivate some new notational devices for writing phonological rules. I have tried to demonstrate the efficacy of these devices, arriving in the process at what I believe to be the appropriate formulation of two rules of Chaha which would otherwise severely strain the formalism. Chaha-internal evidence suggested but did not uniquely determine what these formulations ought to be; cross-linguistic evidence was essential in establishing the new notation.

The proposed notational devices are more restricted than those lying at the foundation of the Chomsky-Halle formalism and at least in part replace them. For expository convenience, however, I have sketched some conventions which translate the new devices into the familiar Chomsky-Halle format, not intending thereby to claim any linguistic significance for this translation process. It is quite possible that the notation proposed here ought to be regarded as primitive rather than "abbreviatory" for the purposes of phonological theory, and that the interpretive conventions presented here are mere mathematical artifacts.

REFERENCES

Anderson, Stephen. 1972. "On nasalization in Sudanese." *Linguistic Inquiry* 3.253-268.

Beeler, Madison. 1970. "Sibilant harmony in Chumash." *International Journal of American Linguistics* 36.14-17.

Chomsky, Noam, and Morris Halle. 1968. *The Sound Pattern of English*. New York: Harper and Row.

Hetzron, Robert. 1971. "Internal labialization in the *tt*-group of Outer South-Ethiopic." *Journal of the American Oriental Society* 91.192-207.

__________. 1975. "The *t*-converb in Western Gurage." AAL, 2.

Howard, Irwin. 1972. "A directional theory of rule application in phonology." *University of Hawaii Working Papers in Linguistics*, vol. 4 no. 7.

Jensen, J.T., and M. Stong-Jensen. 1973. "Ordering and directionality of iterative rules." *Papers in Linguistics* 6.66-90.

Johnson, C. Douglas. 1972. *Formal Aspects of Phonological Description.* The Hague: Mouton.

Kiparsky, Paul. 1968. "How abstract is phonology?" Reprinted by the University of Indiana Linguistics Club.

Leslau, Wolf. 1950. *Ethiopic Documents: Gurage.* (Viking Fund Publications in Anthropology, 14) New York: The Viking Fund.

__________. 1966. *Ethiopians Speak II. Chaha.* (University of California Publications in Near Eastern Studies, 9.) Berkeley and Los Angeles: University of California Press.

__________. 1967. "The impersonal in Chaha." *To Honor Roman Jakobson,* 1159-62. The Hague: Mouton.

__________. 1967-8. "The pseudo-gerundive in Chaha." *Rassegna di Studi Etiopici* 23:27-42.

McCawley, James D. 1971. "On the role of notation in generative phonology." Reproduced by the University of Indiana Linguistics Club.

Polotsky, H.J. 1951. *Notes on Gurage Grammar.* (Oriental Notes and Studies published by the Israel Oriental Society, 2). Jerusalem: The Israel Oriental Society.

Postal, Paul. 1969. "Mohawk vowel doubling." *International Journal of American Linguistics* 36.291-8.

Stanley, Richard. 1967. "Redundancy rules in phonology." *Language* 43.393-436.

Monographic Journals of the Near East Afroasiatic Linguistics 2/2 (March 1975)

This paper is part of the
Proceedings
of the
First North-American Conference on Semitic Linguistics
Santa Barbara, California
March 24-25, 1973

THE t-CONVERB IN WESTERN GURAGE
(THE ROLE OF ANALOGY IN HISTORICAL MORPHOLOGY)

Robert Hetzron

University of California
Santa Barbara, California 93106

Converbs are forms of the verb expressing that the clause containing them is coordinated with the subsequent clause. In Central and Peripheral Western Guarge, there is a form called *t*-converb, made up of a palatalized Jussive stem followed by -*t*(*ä*)- and past tense endings. It is assumed that they come from the original converb form of the pattern CäC*i*C-. This form must have undergone a number of changes, one of them being an assimilation to the jussive pattern. This analogical development has to be situated on a non-surface level, since palatalization has to be imposed on the jussive stem to obtain the proper form.

TABLE OF CONTENTS

1. THE CONVERB

In Ethiopian Semitic,[1] instead of sentence coordination by means of conjunctive particles such as "and," the verb of the non-final conjunct clause is not given full morphological

[1]The Ethiopian Semitic languages are - North-Ethiopic: Geez, Tigrinya, Tigre; South-Ethiopic: Transversal South-Ethiopic with Amharic and Argobba on one side, and Harari and East Gurage

treatment, but is put into the so-called CONVERB-form[2] which, originally (see below) expresses only the person, gender and number of the subject. The intended tense, mood and/or type of subordination (all of them categories marked on the verb) are expressed explicitly only by the verb of the final conjunct clause. The only restriction is that a converb can only be affirmative. Here are some simple examples from Amharic:

bälto hedä	'he ate and left'
bälto yəhedall	'he will eat and leave'
bälto yəhid	'let him eat and leave!'
bälto sihed	'when he ate and left' (tenseless)
bälto əndihed	'so that he may eat and leave'

where the same Sg.3m. form of 'eat' *bälto* is used all over. Its interpretation depends on the form of the final verb, here *hedä* 'to go (away)'. This is the Amharic form of the ORIGINAL CONVERB of Ethiopian Semitic.

In the South-Ethiopian languages other than Amharic and Argobba, a partially tense-marked converb was adopted: past, nonpast or jussive/imperative forms followed by a converbial particle *-m(a)* or *-ane/i* (the latter in East Gurage). This form has been called *m*-CONVERB. For the partial tense-marking and other details, see Hetzron 1972, U.4. and U.7. Yet, within this area, Central and Peripheral Western Gurage (abbreviated hereafter CPWG) have also preserved a form of the original converb, augmented by an element *-tä-*, hence its name *t*-CONVERB. In these languages, the *t*-converb is the only converb to be used before a negative final verb, and, it is found alternatively with a type of *m*-converb before all those affirmative forms that do not refer to a completed act, i.e. before all the forms other than past indicative,[3] including the infinitive.[4]

Table 1 is a table comparing the original converb form of the most archaic language of Ethiopia, Ge'ez, and the conjugation of the *t*-converb in Ezha (Central Western Gurage). The root used

---

(Selti, Wolane, Zway) on the other; and Outer South-Ethiopic subdivided into an *n*-group (Soddo, Goggot and Gafat) and a *tt*-group (Muher and Western Gurage). Western Gurage is divided into Mäsqan and two dialect clusters - Central Western Gurage (Chaha, Ezha, Gumer, Gura) and Peripheral Western Gurage (Ennemor, Gyeto, Endegeñ, Ener). The term Gurage (*gʷəragʷe*) refers to an area where Semitic languages of different affiliations are spoken: East Gurage, Western Gurage, Soddo, Goggot and Muher. For details, see Hetzron 1972.

[2]The traditional name for this morpho-syntactic category is "gerund" (French "gérondif"). This is inappropriate because it is more inspired by the French "literal" rendering of these forms (*en...-ant*) than by the true function of the forms themselves. The term "converb" was introduced by Polotsky (1951:41), primarily for the *m*-converb mentioned below. I find "converb" to be the most adequate term for all the forms.

[3]I mean true past. Before a conditional composed of *bä-*(real)/*tä-*(unreal) + past tense form, the *t*-converb is permissible. The only special case is the durative past composed of a nonpast form + past tense copula, where, either by virtue of the nonpast shape or for semantic reasons (durative, non-completed), the *t*-converb is allowed.

[4]In Leslau's writings, e.g. his 1966 and 1967-8a, this form is called "pseudo-gerundive." First of all, "gerundive" has been shown by Polotsky (1951:41) to be a Gallicism. Yet Polotsky would not object to the term "gerund" for this form (*ibid.*, 45), probably because it does not show tense. But I do not think that any "pseudo-term" has room in linguistic terminology.

for these two is *s-b-r* 'break'. Since the final *r* is subject to modification in CPWG[5], in a third column I am presenting the *t*-converb form of the root *k-t-f* 'chop meat' in Ennemor, a Peripheral Western Gurage language. For another verb class, the *t*-converb of the roots *g-r-z* 'to be(come) old' and *n/r-k/h-β* 'to find' in Ennemor are given in a fourth and fifth columns. The Chaha forms would be almost the same as in Ennemor, except that they would have almost the same endings as in Ezha (Sg.2f. *-h*^{y}, Pl.2/3m/f. *-hu/-hma/-βo/-ma*).

TABLE 1. CONVERB FORMS

	GE'EZ	EZHA	ENNEMOR	ENNEMOR	ENNEMOR
Sg.1c.	*säbirəyyä*	*səbittäh*^{w}	*kətiftäh*^{w}	*gəräžtäh*^{w}	*nəheβtäh*^{w}
2m.	*säbiräkä*	*səbittähä*	*kətiftähä*	*gəräžtähä*	*nəheβtähä*
2f.	*säbiräki*	*səbittäh*^{y}	*kətiftäšua*	*gəräžtäšua*	*nəheβtäšua*
3m.	*säbiro*	*səbittä*	*kətiftä*	*gəräžtä*	*nəheβtä*
3f.	*säbira*	*səbittäč*	*kətiftäč*	*gəräžtäč*	*nəheβtäč*
Pl.1c.	*säbiränä*	*səbittänä*	*kətiftänä*	*gəräžtänä*	*nəheβtänä*
2m.	*säbiräkəm(m?)u*	*səbittähu*	*kətiftähua*	*gəräžtähua*	*nəheβtähua*
2f.	*säbiräkəma*	*səbittähma*	*kətiftähaa*	*gəräžtähaa*	*nəheβtähaa*
3m.	*säbiromu*	*səbittäbo*	*kətiftäua*	*gəräžtäua*	*nəheβtäua*
3f.	*säbiron*	*səbittäma*	*kətiftaa*	*gəräžtaa*	*nəheβtaa*
Impersonal	-	*səbitto*	*kətifto*	*gəräzto*	*nəheβto*

The Ge'ez forms are based on a pattern *CäCiC-ä-*, i.e. a basis of probably nominal origin (cf. the Akkadian stative *kašid*) and an (adverbial) accusative ending *-ä-*, followed by possive suffixes. Amharic has almost the same form: *CäCC-ä-* with somewhat modified possessive suffixes, but with no trace of *-i-*.[6] Tigrinya does not have the accusative ending *-ä-*, but it has the *-i-*: *CäCiC-*. CPWG, on the other hand, has *-i-*, *-e-* or another exponent of palatality (e.g. z → ž above), it also contains the element *-ä-*, but this one is preceded by a *-t-*. This *-t-* is geminated in Ezha, the only CPWG language that has fully preserved the original gemination.[7] An important difference between the two types of converb is that the Ge'ez (and Tigrinya, Amharic, Argobba) converb is conjugated by means of possessive suffixes, whereas CPWG uses the past tense endings, e.g. Sg.1c. *-yyä* vs. *-h*^{w}, Sg.3f. *-a* vs. *-č*. In spite of these differences, it is possible to see that the *t*-converb is a weather-beaten, but still surviving continuation of the original Ethiopian converb.

[5]The conjugation in Ezha given below is what I collected in Ethiopia. Another Ezha speaker interviewed by M.L. Bender gave, for my *səbittä*, a non-assimilated form *səbrəttä*. This is one more indication of the importance of subdialectal research in Ethiopian Semitic. Even the smaller languages exhibit interesting subdialectal variations that may all be relevant historical reconstruction, or important in a synchronic evaluation of syntax and morphology.

[6]Semitic short *i* (and *u*) became Ø~ə in Ethiopian Semitic, while long *i:* became *i* (with no relevant length). Since Amharic is supposed to have preserved the timbre of an original long *i:*, it must be assumed that proto-Semitic had a short *i* here, in agreement with the Akkadian stative pattern *kašid*, but Ge'ez and proto-CPWG lengthened it, to save it from disappearance, for it was functional in the morphophonemic rules.

[7]In my own data, I have one more instance of *t*-converb in Ezha: *orğittä* from *andäm* (Jussive *-ord*) 'put down' (causative of *wrd*). The gemination of the *t* in Ezha is subject to subdialectal variation. The variety of Ezha examined by Polotsky (1938:69, fn.3) has single *t* with no gemination at all, e.g. fn.91: *täzäbbetä* 'return'. In Leslau 1967-8b, the following instances of *t*-converb are found: *oyättoy* 'one puts it down' (No. 28), *täkittoy* 'one

2. THE MORPHOPHONEMICS OF THE *t*-CONVERB IN CHAHA

Before going on to the historical part, let us establish the morphophonemic rules that produce the *t*-converb form in Chaha, the most important Central Western Gurage language. This language is the only one where enough data are available for obtaining a clear image of the situation, thanks to Leslau's detailed study (1967-8a).

It was noticed first by Polotsky that the shape of the *t*-converb can be analyzed as consisting of a base homonymous with the feminine singular imperative (i.e. jussive stem + palatalization, see fn. 15 below), followed by an element *tä*, and conjugated as a past tense form.[8]

2.1. The feminine singular imperative

The morphophonemics of the feminine singular imperative is quite complicated by itself. It uses the jussive stem as a basis to which a palatal element is added. In Ge'ez, the basic degree[9] of the verb has the following two jussive stem patterns. CCC, e.g. *səbər* 'break!',[10] and CCäC, e.g. *rəkäb* 'find!'. These stem forms, used by themselves, are masculine singular imperatives. The corresponding feminine is formed in Ge'ez by the addition of an *-i* (Semitic *-i:*), thus *səbəri* and *rəkäbi* respectively. The jussive is obtained through prefixation of person markers to the stem, combined with the suffixes *-u* for masculine plural and *-a* for feminine plural. The two jussive stem forms, the *səbər*-type and the *rəkäb*-type, have survived in the *tt*-group of Outer South-Ethiopic,[11] which includes CPWG. The suffix *-i*, on the other hand, became absorbed by the stem in a rather complicated manner, and appears as a palatal element imposed on one or two phonemes of the stem.

The following account on the palatalization in the feminine singular imperative is based on Leslau 1967-8a. All the consonants except the labials and *n* are subject to palatalization.

---

cooked it' (No. 63), *nəqittoy* 'one pulls it out' (No. 71), *zarg^y ətta* 'he walks' (No. 107) with geminated *t*, but *wetä* 'he goes' with a single *t*. The first three are impersonal forms followed by the Sg.3m. object suffix *-y*. (Note that the form *baṭṭoy* (No. 47) is not a *t*-converb of the verb *aččäm* 'shut', but a temporal composed of *bä-* 'when' + *-aṭṭo-* Past Impersonal of *-aččä-* + *-y* Sg.3m. object suffix). In the other dialect, examined by Bender, there is *wettä*, also with gemination. It is interesting to note that in this variety of Ezha there is no vowel *i* or *e* in the stem. The forms noted are *səbərettä* for 'break', *kətfəttä* for 'chop meat', *gəräžəttä* for 'be old', *nəhəbəttä* or *nəhäbəttä* for 'find'.

[8]Polotsky 1938:169, fn. 3: 'Le thème verbal apparaît sous une forme qui est identique, extérieurement, à l'impérative fém.sg.; il lui est ajouté un élément *ta-*, conjugué comme parfait', cf. also Polotsky 1951:45 (with Errata on p. 58) and Leslau 1967-8a:28 and 33.

[9]I borrow the term "degree" from Gouffé (1962) to designate what is called *binyan* in Hebrew grammar, "Roman numeral + form" in Arabic, "basic and derived *stems*" in English, i.e. for different verbal uses (voices, etc.) of a root. The term "stem" should refer to a base-form, such as "jussive stem," to which pre- and suffixes may be added, and is thus inappropriate for the designation of deverbal verb derivation, such as "passive," "causative," etc. Leslau used the Gallicism "theme" for this, but French *thème* means exactly the same as "stem."

[10]The vowel [ə] is nonphonemic and its presence is conditioned by the consonant clustering (and sometimes by other factors).

[11]See Leslau 1951. This is one more isogloss justifying the division of Outer South-Ethiopic into a *tt*-group and an *n*-group. In the South-Ethiopic languages other than the *tt*-group, the *rəkäb*-type was generalized. Furthermore, Soddo and Goggot change the stem vowel *ä* into *ə* after a preceding *ä*, e.g. *yäsbər* 'let him break!' vs. *təsbär* 'let her break!'.

The following actual changes constitute palatalization: *d* → *ǧ*, *t* → *č*, *ṭ* → *č̣*, *z* → *ž*, *s* → *š*, *g* → *g*ʸ, *k* → *k*ʸ, *q* → *q*ʸ, *h* → *h*ʸ, *r* → *y*.[12] The base may already contain palatal consonants: *ǧ*, *č*, *č̣*, *ž*, *š*. In this case, palatalization applies vacuously in that it occasions no phonetic modification.

The palatalization imposed on the basic jussive stem may be non-formally described by means of the following statements (using P as a symbol for Palatalization):

(I) If the stem ends in an -*a*, this one becomes -*ä* or -*æ*, e.g. *wəṭa*+P → *wəč̣ä* 'go out', *səma*+P → *simä*/*simæ* 'hear' (where one can also see the effects of (II) and (IV) respectively).

(II) If the last consonant of the stem is other than a labial or *n*, it becomes palatalized, e.g. *nəmäd*+P → *nəmäǧ* 'love', *wətäq*+P → *wətäq*ʸ 'fall', *gəräz*+P → *gəräž* 'be(come) old', *nəkəs*+P → *nəkəš* 'bite', *gəfər*+P → *gəfi* 'let go', *bəhär*+P → *bəhe* 'lack, miss' (see (VII) below). Vacuous application: *fəǧ*+P → *fəǧ* 'destroy', *mač*+P → *mač* 'be(come) angry'.

(III) If the second last consonant of the stem is identical with the last one (but is not *r*), and this one has undergone (II), the second last one is also palatalized: *səkək*+P → *sək*ʸ*ək*ʸ 'plant into the ground', *ädəd*+P → *äǧəǧ* 'cut peas', *äsəs*+P → *äšəš* 'sweep', *nəzäz*+P → *nəžäž* 'dream', *bätət*+P → *báčəč* 'be wide'.

(IV) When the last consonant of the stem is *n*, no change takes place: *ṭän*+P → *ṭän* 'give birth to', *m*ʷ*an*+P → *m*ʷ*an* 'be jealous'.[13] Another instance of no change is *ṭəw*+P → *ṭəw* 'suck'. Since I have no other example of final *w*, I cannot tell whether it is due to the *w* or to some other factor.

(V) When the last consonant is a labial stop (Polotsky 1951:23), the vowel before it is palatalized: *ə*+P → *i*, *a*/*ä*+P → *e*, e.g. *səma*+P → *simä* 'hear', *gədəf*+P → *gədif* 'break the fast', *nəhäβ*+P → *nəheβ* 'find', *səräf*+P → *səref* 'fear', *šaβ*+P → *šeβ* 'pull'. The pre-labial palatalization has to be stated in terms of vowels in view of the following: *agβa*+P → *ag*ʸ*βä* 'marry', *aṭfa*+P → *aṭifä* 'destroy'. *ag*ʸ*βä* is the practical equivalent of *agiβä* (cf. (VII)), and *aṭifä* has a vowel and is not **ač̣fä*. Possibly, the palatal element should be represented as *y* in order to trigger *šwa*-insertion - *aṭfa*+P → *aṭyfä* → *aṭəyfä* → *aṭifä*.

(VI) If the last two consonants are identical labials (and (V) has been executed), and the initial (third last) consonant is back, this one is further palatalized: *qəfef*+P → *q*ʸ*əfif* 'cut edges', *həβəβ*+P → *h*ʸ*əβiβ* 'surround', cf. *ṭəməm*+P → *ṭəmim* 'be crooked (shape)', with no change in the initial consonant.

---

[12] In his description, Leslau confuses the palatalization occasioned by the feminine singular and the formation of its basis: the jussive stem. Thus, his 6-8 on p. 34 are completely misrepresented. There is no *əna-i* → *əyä*, but *əra-i* → *əyä*, which can be taken care of by other rules. *n*~*r* corresponds to past tense stem~jussive stem. Likewise, instead of *gən-i*, read *gər-i*; instead of *gənəf-i*, the correct starting point is *gərəf-i*. Similarly, on p. 38, the depalatalization of the root is not due to the *t*-converb formation *gäkəčtä* < *g*ʸ*äk*ʸ*ätäm* 'accompany', but is a property of the jussive stem *gäkət* which, then, undergoes another type of palatalization. Naturally, interrelating the jussive stem and the other two: past and nonpast, is also a very interesting and challenging problem.

[13] The behavior of the *n* might be historically explained by the assumption that there had originally been a *ɲ* in this position which vacuously underwent (II). Later all *ɲ* became *n* in Central Western Gurage (Hetzron 1972, I.2d.). For the verb 'come' Mäsqan actually has a jussive stem *täɲ*, and for 'give birth' Ennemor has *ʔäɲ* (with *ṭ*>*ʔ*) and for 'jealous' *m*ʷ*aɲä*, all three still with the original *ɲ*.

(VII) Finally, there are a few general assimilation rules: *ä+y → e*, *a+y → e*, and *ə+y → i*,[14] which contribute to the formation of feminine singular imperatives (following *r → y*), e.g. *bəhär+P → bəhäy → bəhe* 'lack, miss', *dar+P → day → de* 'bless', *səβər+P → səβəy → səβi* 'break'. Note further that there is neutralization between Back Consonant + *i* and Back Consonant^y + *ə* (for Amharic, see Tubiana 1968). Thus, what Leslau describes as *nəg^{y}əf* 'fall down', *nəq^{y}əm* 'pick up' are basically not different from *nəgif* and *nəqim* resulting from (V). On a phonetic plane, back consonants are very easily palatalized, so that the first type of realization is more common.

The above is a plain description of the facts. For a formalized presentation of the phenomenon, see Johnson's study in this same journal.

The other CPWG languages have almost the same system as Chaha. Unfortunately, the data available are incomplete, and no adequate statement can be made at this time about them. In fn. 7 I have signalled the existence of a dialect of Ezha that never has a palatal VOWEL as a result of this palatalizing process, thus (V) above does not apply. A more important divergence from Chaha is found in Ennemor. The verbs with weak mid radicals have a segmental final *-i*. While for Chaha *šaβ* 'pull' there is *šaβ+P → šeβ*, Ennemor gives such a root a different treatment: *šaam+P → šaami*. Ennemor also allows the diphthong *ay*, e.g. Chaha *e-säβər*, Ennemor *a-ysäβər(-ka)* 'he does not break', thus for Chaha *dar+P → de* 'bless', Ennemor has *daar+P → daay*.

2.2. The formation of the *t*-converb

As pointed out above, the *t*-converb is formed out of a base homonymous with the feminine singular imperative, through the addition of an element *tä* and past tense endings. This element is *ttä* in Ezha (fn. 7) and a mere *t* in Gumär. Thus, the Sg.1c. form of *k-t-f* 'chop meat' is *kətiftäh^w* in Chaha and Ennemor, but *kətfəttäh^w* in Ezha and *kətiftəh^w* in Gumär.

The personal endings are the same as after the past tense. It is, nevertheless, remarkable that Pl.3m. has *-βo* in Chaha and *-bo* in Ezha, as against the normal Pl.3m. ending after the past: *-o*. The ending *-βo/-bo* is used in these languages in the past after verbs with weak final radicals, e.g. Ezha *säbbär-o-* 'they (masc.) broke', vs. *nättä-bo-* 'they tore off'. Finally, against Ennemor *səβiitäh^w* (Sg.1c. of 'break'), Endegeñ has *siiča*, where *-ča* may come from **-t-ya*, while the other personal endings are like in Ennemor. This has great historical importance (see below).

3. THE ORIGIN OF THE *t*-CONVERB

3.0. Confrontation with the Original Converb

It would, of course, be absurd to assume that historically the *t*-converb has anything to do with the feminine singular imperative.[15] The latter is a derived form itself, the jussive

[14] These rules do not apply before vowels, as there are words like *gäpäyä* 'brother', *äyaž* 'he does not see', *əya* 'I', *yəqəyä* 'he waits'. Some further examples of the application of these rules: *tə+ysäβər* (šwa epenthesis) → *tisäβər* 'when he breaks', *a + ysäβər → esäβər* 'he does not break' (*a-* negative prefix as in *atsäβər* 'she does not break'), and with the Sg:3m. object suffix *-y*: *yəsäwr+y → yəsäwrəy* (šwa rule) → *yəsäwri* 'one breaks it', *nəsäβənnä+y → nəsäβənne* 'we break it', *yəsäβräma+y → yəsäβräme* 'they (fem.) break it'.

[15] This can be proved with certainty. In Chaha, like in many Afro-asiatic (Hamito-Semitic) languages, the imperative of the verb 'come' is suppletive, - for the past tense *čänä-* / non-past *-čän* / jussive *-tän*, the imperative of Sg.masc. *nehä*, fem. *neh^y*, Pl.masc. *nehu*, fem. *nehma*. If the *t*-converb were really based on the femine IMPERATIVE, one would expect **neh^{y}tä*, which is not the right form. The *t*-converb of 'come' is *täntä*, based on the jussive stem.

stem with palatalization imposed on it, representing an older Sg.2f. suffix *-i:*. What is, then the connection between the jussive stem and the *t*-converb on the one hand, and where is the palatalization coming from, on the other?

It has already been suggested above that the *t*-converb is historically related to the original converb form, of the pattern *CäCiC-ä-* in the basic degree, as attested in Ge'ez, which, in turn, is connected with the Akkadian stative *CaCiC*. Yet, there are non-negligible differences between the CPWG *kətiftä/nəheßtä* patterns and the original *kätifä*-type. Let us review the differences found between the two in the basic degree of the sound verbs:

A. The vowel between the first two radicals is *ä* (< short *a*) in Ge'ez, but *ə* in CPWG.

B. The vowel between the second and third radicals is always *i* in Ge'ez, whereas in CPWG it can also be *e*.[16]

C. The third radical is followed in CPWG by a *t* (Ezha *tt*), but not in Ge'ez.

D. CPWG uses past tense endings for person marking (but Pl.3m. *-ßo/-bo* instead of *-o*), whereas the original converb (Ge'ez, Tigrinya, Amharic, Argobba) has possessive endings.

Do these differences constitute enough reason for rejecting the idea of any connection between the two, or can a reasonable and plausible hypothesis be found which would explain the divergence in an acceptable manner? In Hetzron 1972, U.3b. I advanced such a hypothesis. The following is an elaboration of what I already said.

3.1. The Element *t*

In Argobba (Leslau 1959:262-3), the converb forms are augmented by an element *d*, e.g. *säbrədo*, Sg.3m. converb corresponding to Amharic *säbro*, Ge'ez *säbiro*. The *-d-* can be traced back to an older *-t*, the voicing of an original final *-t* being a fairly regular (though not exceptionless) phenomenon in Argobba (cf. Leslau 1952:252, mistakenly labeled "devoicing," see also Leslau 1967-8a:27, fn.3). The element *t* was identified by Leslau (1959:263) with the *t* that appears in the Amharic converb (and infinitive) of verbs with final weak radical, e.g. *sämto* Sg.3m. converb of *sämma* 'hear' (inf. *mäsmat*, Argobba *mäsmit*),[17] which was, in Argobba, extended to all the verbs. Even though CPWG exhibits no such spurious *t* in the infinitive of these verbs (e.g. Chaha *wäsma* 'hear'),[18] it is still possible that this *t* had existed in both contexts and was, as in Argobba, generalized in the converb (not unlike in the infinitive, cf. fn. 18). In the context of Semitic, it is also imaginable that if the basic pattern *sabir* was a nominal form (followed by an adverbial accusative to form a converb), the shape that underlay CPWG and Argobba converbs was the corresponding feminine **sabirt* (the Ethiopian feminine is typically *-t* and not *-at*). This would also explain the positioning of the case-ending after it: **säbirt-ä-*.

---

[16]Here we can temporarily disregard the fact that the *i/e*+Labial is, patternwise, equivalent to *ə/ä*+Palatalized consonant, e.g. *nəheß-* vs. *gəräž-*, cf. 3.4.

[17]Most probably related to the *t* appearing in Hebrew IIIy verbs, e.g. *rāṣāh* 'he wanted', prepositional infinitive *-rṣōt*.

[18]But Gafat, another Outer South-Ethiopic tongue, does: *wäsmət* (?, Leslau 1956:123). Note that Central Western Gurage has two alternative shapes for the infinitive, *wä*+jussive stem, or jussive stem+*ot*, and in Peripheral Western Gurage the only infinitive is derived from the second type (Hetzron 1971). Geez has an infinitive ending in *-o* in the derived degrees, alternating with *-ot* (also appearing optionally in the basic degree) mainly before suffixes. While *-ōt* is confined in Hebrew to IIIy verbs (there is *-t* also in the most frequent Iy verbs), *-ot* was generalized for all the verb classes in Ethiopian.

3.2. Assimilation to the Past Tense Forms

We can find a unitary explanation for the other major differences between the original converb and the *t*-converb: the vowel ə in the first syllable (in the basic degree): A in 3.0., - for the past tense endings: D, and for the Pl.3m. suffix -*βo*/-*bo* (as against the normal -*o*): 2.2., and, finally, also for the gemination of the *t* in Ezha (fn. 7).

In Amharic, for example, different types of morphs are used for the expression of the subject: subject markers proper *ə-säbər* ('I break', base form), *säbbär-hu* ('I broke'); object suffixes *nä-ɲɲ* (copula: 'I am'); possessive endings *säbər-r-e* (Sg.1c. converb). In the Gurage languages (taken as an area), on the other hand, one finds that object and possessive suffixes had been eliminated from the function of subject-marking.[19] Against Amharic *nä-ɲɲ*, Gafat *nä-y* (*ɲ* → *y*) and Harari *intä-ɲ*, the other South-Ethiopic languages have past tense endings in the copula: *nä-hʷ*/*n-hʷ*/*n-ku*. It is the same trend that changed the **säbirt-ya* type, with the possessive ending, to **säbirtä-hʷ*. Endegeñ has a curious form for the Sg.1c. converb: *siiča*, which may very well be a survival of the old form with still the possessive ending.

The reorganization of the converb form according to the past tense explains the rest. The base to which the suffix was attached was **säbirtä-* with a vocalic ending. Such an ending is found in verbs with final weak radical that require, in Central Western Gurage, the Pl.3m. suffix -*βo*/-*bo* (as against the usual -*o*). The converb consequently adopted the same suffix by analogy.[20] Among the CPWG languages Ezha is the only one that completely preserved consonantal gemination. In this language, the second to last radical of a past tense form is geminated. This explains why it developed for the converb, in the process of being reshaped according to the past tense, the form *səbrəttä-* (where -*ä*- is taken to be the final, weak radical). Finally, in this pattern, there are more than three pseudo-radicals involved, the three true radicals + *t*(*t*) + *ä*. This explains *ä* → *ə* in the initial syllable. The past tense stem of quadriradical roots is of the pattern *mäskär-* in North-Ethiopic. Because of the generalization of penultimate gemination in the past tense forms, South-Ethiopic developed *mäsäkkär-*, still so in Amharic, Argobba and Gafat. The languages in the far south, Harari and all of Gurage, shortened the initial *ä* to *ə*: *məsäkkär-* (Harari -*i*-). It is the same shortening that affected the original form of **säbirtä-* and made it *səbirtä-*. With the final -*ä* that had a radical value, this form behaved as a quadriradical.[21] In other terms, proto-CPWG developed a morpheme-structure restriction requiring a vowel *ə* (instead of the older *ä*) in the antepenultimate syllable of a stem that is followed by past tense endings, and this change is nothing more than abiding by this restriction.

3.3. The Jussive Stem

The vowel between the second and third radicals is *i* when the corresponding jussive stem has an ə, e.g. *kətiftä* (jussive -*ktəf*), and it is *e* when the jussive has *ä* (cf. Leslau 1951), e.g. *nəheβtä* (jussive -*nhäβ*). This indicates that the input to palatalization, as described in 2.1., is always the jussive stem of the verb. This can also be confirmed by verbs with initial palatal consonants that are depalatalized in the jussive: Ennemor *žäpär'ä* 'he returned (tr.)', jussive stem -*zäpər*, *t*-converb *zäpitä*; *täžäpär'ä* 'he returned (intr.)', jussive stem -*t*(*ä*)*zäpär*, *t*-converb *täzäpetä*. Another form based on the jussive stem in CPWG is the infinitive (cf. fn. 18 above).

---

[19]The beginnings of this tendency are already manifested in Amharic where 'she is' is either *nat* with an object suffix or *näč* with a past tense ending.

[20]Or, in a more formalized account, if the Pl.3m. past tense ending spelling rule produces -*o* after consonant and -*βo*/-*bo* after vowel, it is no wonder that -*βo*/-*bo* was adopted after the final vowel of the converb stem.

[21]One might also say a "quinquiradical," but if and constituted one cluster, they may not have been considered separate elements in the radical count. At any rate, this is immaterial.

Let us take a look at the converb form in different degrees, compared with the infinitive in jussive stems, in Ge'ez which represents an archaic type (though not ancestral to CPWG):

DEGREE	CONVERB		INFINITIVE		JUSSIVE STEM
basic	*säbir-ä-*	=	*säbir*		*-sbər/-rkäb*
geminate	*säbbir-ä-*	~	*säbbər-o*	=	*-säbbər*
causative	*asbir-ä-*	~	*asbər-o*	=	*-asbər*
passive	*täsäbir-ä-*	~	*täsäbr-o*		*-täsäbär*

We can notice the identity of the infinitive and jussive stems in the geminate and causative degrees (marked by '='). The converbs have, in all the degrees, a vowel *-i-* between the last two radicals. Thus, the converb stems may be represented as based on the infinitive stem, with an added closed palatal vowel (this is marked by '~'), also found in the basic infinitive (marked by '='). In the passive, the jussive has the vowel *-ä-* characteristic of all the prefix-conjugated passive forms, which makes this case divergent from the other two forms. Now, already in Amharic one finds that by the analogy of the jussive stem *-ssäbär* (with assimilation of *-t-*), the infinitive also adopted the same *-ä-*: *mässäbär* 'to be broken', but not yet the converb: *täsäbr-ä-*. This indicates a general levelling off tendency between the jussive and the infinitive in the whole of South-Ethiopic, in which proto-CPWG must also have taken part. If the converb form was actually derived in proto-CPWG, through *i*-insertion, from the infinitive stem, it must have followed the latter in adapting to the jussive stem and become **täsäbä+i+r-tä* → **täsäbertä* (→ *täsäβetä*). Here is a graphic representation of what can be reconstructed:

ANALOGICAL DEVELOPMENTS IN THE PASSIVE DEGREE

CONVERB	INFINITIVE	JUSSIVE STEM	
täsäb(i)r-ä-	*täsäbr-o(t)*	*-täsäbär*	(Ge'ez, proto-Eth., fn. 6)
täsäb(+i+)r-ä	*-t(ä)säbär*	*-t(ä)säbär*	(proto-South Eth.)[22]
täsäbä+i+r-(t)ä-	*-tsäbär*	*-t(ä)säbär*	(proto-CPWG)

In the South-Ethiopic languages other than the *tt*-group, the basic jussive stem became a generalized *-sbär*, which pattern was, as in the case of the passive, imposed on the infinitive, e.g. Amharic *mäsbär* 'to break'. In the *tt*-languages, where both types of jussive stem were maintained, the same analogical development produced the infinitive forms (Chaha) *wä-sβər*/*wä-rhäβ* (*n-* ~ *-r*). The assimilation of the *t*-converb form to the past tense forms, as described in 3.2., changed an older **säbirtä-/räkibtä-* to **səbirtä-/rəkibtä-* with a base *səbir-/rəkib-* where the first one, *səbir*, automatically conformed to the morphophonemic rule already valid for all the other degrees: infinitive + palatal vowel = converb form. The only diverging form, **rəkib-tä-* ≠ jussive *rəkäb* was adapted to this situation, thus **rəkä+i+b-tä-* → **rəkebtä* (→ *nəheβtä*). Graphically represented:

[22] For the converb, no more *i* in proto-Amharic/Argobba, but, like in North-Ethiopic, proto-Outer South-Ethiopic had a lengthening of the *i* (which saved it from complete disappearance). In Amharic, the group *t*C (here *ts*) became CC (here *ss*).

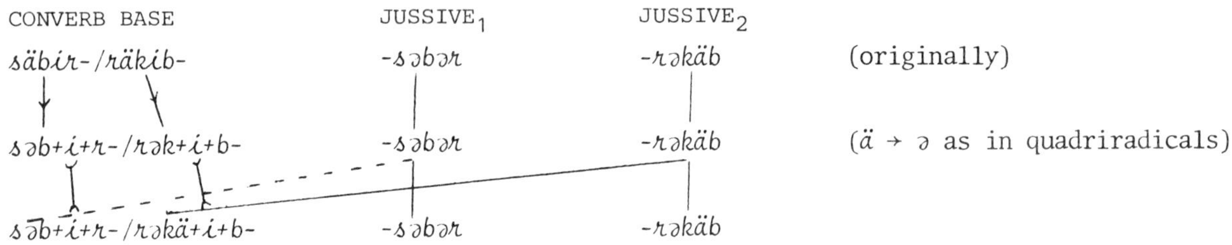

where the interrupted line indicates analogy observed, and the arrowed line the analogical change due to the assimilation to a quadriradical past tense form.

3.4. The Palatalization

We have ended up with a jussive stem that has an additional palatal vowel between the last two radicals. The palatality imposed on the vowel that is found in that position. One finds that affixal labial and palatal elements came to be observed by the stem in CPWG, as supra-segmental elements, e.g. *yəčäkər* 'he cooks' + **u* (orginally Pl.3m., later impersonal ending) became *yəčäkʷər-* 'one cooks' (Hetzron 1971). Suffixal palatal vowels were absorbed to a lesser extent in that they could not "travel" as far from the end of the word as labiality. The infixal palatality in the converb was also absorbed, and in doing so it adopted the same morphophonemic rules of palatalization as the Sg.2f. form of the nonpast (e.g. *təräkəs+*i* → *təräkəš* 'you (fem.) bite') and the imperative (*nəkəš* 'bite' (fem.)!' from old **nəkəs+i*), for example *nəkəštä* (from older infixal **nəkə+i+š-tä*).

3.5. Recapitulation

The original converb form of the pattern "*säbir-ä* + Possessive endings" underwent the following changes (basic degree):

(1) A *t* was inserted right after the stem: *säbir-t-ä-*;

(2) The form was reorganized after the past tense forms, as a quadriradical verb with a weak final radical, **säbirtä*-Poss. → **səbirtä*-Past endings (Pl.3m. *-bo*) (→ *səbərəttä*-Past endings in Ezha).[23]

(3) The initial *ə*, replacing the original *ä*, made the stem more similar to the jussive, hence the analogical development: **səbirtä-/rəkibtä-* (cf. jussive *-səbər/-rəkäb*) → **səbirtä-/rəkəbtä-* (→ *səβitä/nəhəβtä*). In other terms, - reorganization of the input of the palatalization according to the jussive stem in conformity with the situation in the other degrees.

(4) The palatal element, originally infixed between the last two radicals, merged with the root palatalization (2.1.) of the originally suffixal Sg.2f. marker.

4. THEORETICAL IMPLICATIONS

The above reconstructed history of the *t*-converb may or may not be accepted. Let me point out, however, that efficiently rejecting it would also require a plausible counter-hypothesis that can account for all the facts equally well as, or better than, the one proposed above. I cannot see how this could be done.[24] But the main point is that the adoption/rejection of the

[23] Like a verb of the *zərägg ʸä*-class. Note that many of these "abbreviated" quadriradicals contain a palatalized consonant, a souvenir of the old final radical **y* (e.g. **zngy*). This made the analogy with the palatalized converb even more at hand.

[24] See note 15 for a powerful argument against the possibility that the *t*-converb was remodeled directly after the feminine singular imperative, which would completely invalidate the main point here.

present hypothesis is not a function of adherence to such or such linguistic schools. Its plausibility may be weighed by general criteria.

The correlation between the jussive patterns *-ktəf/-nhäβ* and the *t*-converb patterns *kətif(tä)/nəheβ(tä)* is conspicuous (in the derived degrees just as much). Now, if one accepts the idea of historical relationship between the old, original converb *kätif-ä-/näkib-ä-* and the new *t*-converb *kətiftä-/nəheβtä-*, one has to posit a reorganization of the forms under the analogical influence of the jussive, summed up by the proportion:

i : *e* = *ə* : *ä*

The *t*-converb contains palatalization which is not part of the jussive (cf. fn. 15 for the actual role of the feminine imperative). Therefore, the analogy can be understood only if situated on a non-surface level, preceding palatalization, namely (for the vowel between the last two radicals):

NON-SURFACE ANALOGY

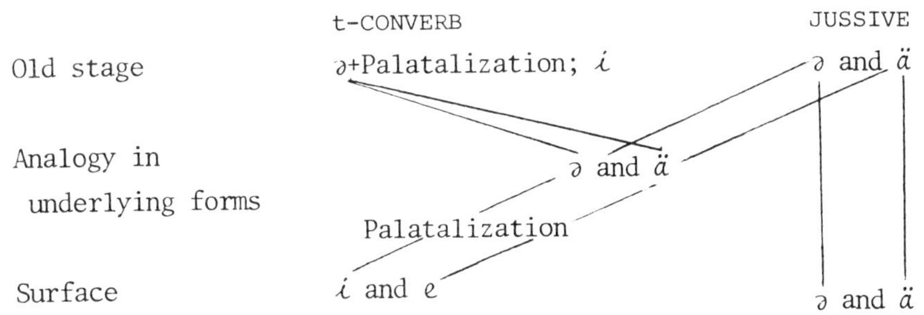

One may object that the concept of "proportionate analogy" as summed up by the formula *i:e=ə:ä* provides another explanation for this development, without any recourse to the concept of "non-surface," i.e. underlying level. But one also has to realize that such a proportion is only an abbreviated, contracted notation of the same thing. The notion of "identity" which appears in statements about analogy is easy to capture (e.g. passage from non-identity to identity). Identity of a concrete idea. On the other hand, proportionate analogy involves abstraction. In the present case, it states that if the palatality feature were not present (in *i* and *e*), we would have in the *t*-converb respectively the same vowels as in the corresponding jussive (ə and *ä*). Extracting palatality in such a manner is a deviation from a strictly surface representation, and its philosophy implies that palatality is superimposed on other, more basic vowels. And this is what "underlying vs. surface" is all about.

REFERENCES

Gouffé, Claude. 1962. 'Observations sur le degré causatif dans un parler haoussa du Niger', *Journal of African Languages*, 1.182-200.

Hetzron, Robert. 1964. 'La voyelle du sixième ordre en amharique', *Journal of African Languages*, 3.179-90.

Hetzron, Robert. 1970. 'Vocalic length and stress in Ennemor', *Le Muséon*, 83.559-81.

Hetzron, Robert. 1971. 'Internal Labialization in the *tt*-group of Outer South-Ethiopic', *Journal of the American Oriental Society*, 91.192-207.

Hetzron, Robert. 1972. *Ethiopian Semitic, Studies in classification.* The Manchester University Press.

Johnson, C. Douglas. 1975. 'Phonological channels in Chaha', AAL 2/2.

Leslau, Wolf. 1950. *Ethiopic documents: Gurage.* New York: The Viking Fund.

Leslau, Wolf. 1951. 'Le type *läbsä* en gouragué'. *Rassegna di studi etiopici*, 10.85-98.

Leslau, Wolf. 1956. *Étude descriptive et comparative du gafat.* Paris: Klincksieck.

Leslau, Wolf. 1959. 'A preliminary description of Argobba', *Annales d'Éthiopie*, 3.251-73.

Leslau, Wolf. 1966. *Ethiopian speak, Studies in cultural background. II. Chaha.* Berkeley: The University of California Press.

Leslau, Wolf. 1967-8a. 'The pseudo-gerundive in Čaha', *Rassegna di studi etiopici*, 23.27-42.

Leslau, Wolf. 1967-8b. 'Eža riddles', *Rassegna di studi etiopici*, 23.43-78.

Leslau, Wolf. 1970. 'The *ma*-clause in Harari', pp. 263-73 in David Cohen, ed., *Mélanges Marcel Cohen.* The Hague: Mouton.

Tubiana, Joseph. 1968. 'Double neutralisation phonologique en amharique', *Revue de l'École Nationale des Langues Orientales*, 5.85-96.

Polotsky, H.J. 1938. 'Études de grammaire gouragué', *Bulletin de la Société de Linguistique de Paris*, 39.137-75.

Polotsky, H.J. 1951. *Notes on Gurage grammar.* Jerusalem: The Israel Oriental Society.

FIRST NORTH-AMERICAN CONFERENCE ON SEMITIC LINGUISTICS

Santa Barbara, California
March 24-25, 1973

The first North-American Conference on Semitic Linguistics was organized by Robert Hetzron (University of California, Santa Barbara) with the cooperation of Giorgio Buccellati (University of California, Los Angeles) and Joseph L. Malone (Barnard College--Columbia University). The purpose of the Conference is to promote the interest of Semitists in the various modern currents of linguistics. The full list of the papers presented at the 1973 Conference is given below. Those papers which have been submitted and accepted for inclusion in *AAL*, like the present one, are being published within the framework of the journal.

A. *Semitic and its Afroasiatic Cousins*

1. Carleton T. Hodge (University of Indiana), *The Nominal Sentence in Semitic* (=*AAL* 2/4).
2. G. Janssens (University of Ghent, Belgium), *The Semitic Verbal System* (=*AAL* 2/4).
3. J. B. Callender (UCLA), *Afroasiatic Cases and the Formation of Ancient Egyptian Verbal Constructions with Possessive Suffixes* (forthcoming in *AAL*).
4. Russell G. Schuh (UCLA), *The Chadic Verbal System and its Afroasiatic Nature* (forthcoming in *AAL*).
5. Andrzej Zaborski (University of Cracow, Poland), *The Semitic External Plural in an Afroasiatic Perspective* (forthcoming in *AAL*).

B. *Ancient Semitic Languages*

6. Giorgio Buccellati (UCLA), *On the Akkadian "Attributive" Genitive* (=*AAL* 2/9).
7. Daniel Ronnie Cohen (Columbia University), *Subject and Object in Biblical Aramaic: A Functional Approach Based on Form-Content Analysis* (=*AAL* 2/1).
8. Richard Steiner (Touro College, N.Y.), *Evidence from a Conditioned Sound Change for Lateral ḏ in Pre-Aramaic.*
9. Stanislav Segert (UCLA), *Verbal Categories of Some Northwest Semitic Languages: A Didactical Approach* (=*AAL* 2/5).
10. Charles Krahmalkov (University of Michigan), *On the Noun with Heavy Suffixes in Punic.*

C. *Hebrew*

11. Joseph L. Malone (Barnard College--Columbia University), *Systematic vs. Autonomous Phonemics and the Hebrew Grapheme "dagesh"* (=*AAL* 2/7).
12. Allan D. Corré (University of Wisconsin, Milwaukee), *"Wāw" and "Digamma"* (=*AAL* 2/7).
13. Harvey Minkoff (Hunter College, N.Y.), *A Feature Analysis of the Development of Hebrew Cursive Scripts* (=*AAL* 1/7).
14. Raphael Nir (Hebrew University, Jerusalem), *The Survival of Obsolete Hebrew Words in Idiomatic Expressions* (=*AAL* 2/3).
15. Talmy Givón (UCLA), *On the Role of Perceptual Clues in Hebrew Relativization* (=*AAL* 2/9).
16. Alan C. Harris (UCLA), *The Relativization "which that is" in Israeli Hebrew.*

D. *Arabic*

17. Ariel A. Bloch (University of California, Berkeley), *Direct and Indirect Relative Clauses in Arabic.*
18. Frederic J. Cadora (Ohio State University), *Some Features of the Development of Telescoped Words in Arabic Dialects and the Status of Koiné II.*

E. *Ethiopian*

19. Gene B. Gragg (University of Chicago), *Morpheme Structure Conditions and Underlying Form in Amharic* (forthcoming in *AAL*).
20. C. Douglas Johnson (University of California, Santa Barbara), *Phonological Channels in Chaha* (=*AAL* 2/2).
21. Robert Hetzron (University of California, Santa Barbara), *The t-Converb in Western Gurage and the Role of Analogy in Historical Morphology* (=*AAL* 2/2).

F. *Beyond Afroasiatic*

22. Gilbert B. Davidowitz (New York), *Cognate Afroasiatic and Indoeuropean Affixes: Conjugational Person-Markers.*

ASSUR

ASSUR is meant to serve the needs of the specialized field which is closely identified with the study of Assyrian as a dialect of Akkadian and with the history of Assyria as a special aspect of Mesopotamian civilization, from early times down to the end of the Assyrian empire. Given the intensity of linguistic and historical exchanges with neighboring regions, it is clear that the study of Assyrian dialect and history cannot be carried on in isolation, without due consideration to influences deriving from contacts with other people. Hence, ASSUR will also accept articles which are not exclusively Assyrian in scope, as long as they are related to Assyria and useful for the study of its language and history.

Editors: K.-H. Deller, P. Garelli, C. Saporetti
(Address correspondence to Dr. C. Saporetti, Via Vasanello 20, Cassia, 00189 Roma, Italy)

Volume 1

Issue 1: S. Parpola, *The Alleged Middle/Neo-Assyrian Irregular Verb *naṣṣ and the Assyrian Sound Change /š/ > /s/*

Forms of the alleged irregular and defective verb **naṣṣ*, reconstructed as occurring in Middle and Neo-Assyrian texts, are in fact to be understood as forms of the verb *našû*–and hence **naṣṣ* is to be stricken from the dictionaries. The argumentation is based on five considerations. (1) Forms assigned to *našû* and **naṣṣ* respectively are in perfect complementary distribution: missing forms of *našû* are covered by **naṣṣ* and vice versa. (2) Semantically, both verbs are used in exactly the same function. (3) The paradigm is morphologically perfect in the sense that all forms of **naṣṣ* conform to the paradigm of *našû* as known from the Old Assyrian period (in which no forms of **naṣṣ* are attested). (4) There is firm evidence for the validity of the change /š/ > /s/ in the phonological system of Neo-Assyrian. (5) Writings with <*ṣa*> and <*ṣu*> stand for phonemic /*ssa*/ and /*ssu*/.

Issue 2: C. Saporetti, *Some Considerations on the Stelae of Assur*

The publication of new texts has led to the identification of some of the eponyms mentioned in the steles of Assur. An analysis of the data results in a negative conclusion with regard to the possibility of arranging the steles in groups characterized by internal chronological coherence. The original sequence has been lost, and even within the same group there are steles dated to disparate periods, even if they are all Middle-Assyrian. Possibly, a subdivision may be suggested between the steles placed to the North, which may be rather late, and those placed to the South, which may be dated to the period of greatest power–but this differentiation might be accidental.

Issue 3: F. M. Fales, *Notes on Some Nineveh Horse Lists*

The article contains new documentary evidence on horses in Neo-Assyrian times, including the copies, transliterations and translations of three hitherto unpublished and four other texts from Nineveh. The discussion of the data provides an analysis of the internal structure and the nature of the texts. In one group, the horses are classified according to their color, sex and (possibly) age; these texts probably represent the preliminary listing of incoming animals, drawn up for internal use by the administrative unit of the palace in charge of horses. Another group consists of memoranda on specific quantities of horses, which are reports sent daily to the king by the same administrative unit, to provide an "ephemeral" (i.e. not destined to archival files) account of events.